Nifty Thrifty Crafts for Kids

Nifty Thrifty

MUSIC

Crafts

Felicia Lowenstein Niven

Enslow Elementary

an imprint of

Enslow Publishers, Inc.

40 Industrial Road
Box 398
Berkeley Heights, NJ 07922
USA

http://www.enslow.com

Enslow Elementary, an imprint of Enslow Publishers, Inc.

Enslow Elementary® is a registered trademark of Enslow Publishers, Inc.

Library of Congress Cataloging-in-Publication Data

Niven, Felicia Lowenstein.

   Nifty thrifty music crafts / Felicia Lowenstein Niven.

     p. cm. — (Nifty thrifty crafts for kids)

   Includes index.

   ISBN-13: 978-0-7660-2784-8

   ISBN-10: 0-7660-2784-8

     1. Handicraft—Juvenile literature. 2. Musical instruments—Construction—Juvenile literature. I. Title.

II. Series.

TT160.N58 2006

745.5—dc22

                               2006006689

Printed in the United States of America

10 9 8 7 6 5 4 3 2 1

To Our Readers: We have done our best to make sure all Internet Addresses in this book were active and appropriate when we went to press. However, the author and the publisher have no control over and assume no liability for the material available on those Internet sites or on other Web sites they may link to. Any comments or suggestions can be sent by e-mail to comments@enslow.com or to the address on the back cover.

Every effort has been made to locate all copyright holders of material used in this book. If any errors or omissions have occurred, corrections will be made in future editions of this book.

Illustration Credits: Crafts prepared by June Ponte; photography by Nicole diMella/Enslow Publishers, Inc.; © 2006 Jupiterimages, pp. 9 (image on cereal box); 25 (image on cereal box); Shutterstock, pp. 4, 5 (top and bottom).

Cover Illustration: Photography by Nicole diMella/Enslow Publishers, Inc.

Safety Note: Be sure to ask for help from an adult, if needed, to complete these crafts!

Contents

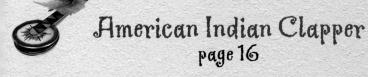
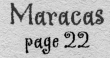
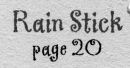

Music!

Music is older than just about anything. Humans probably made music before they spoke. They created musical instruments long before they wrote words.

The first instruments were simple. They were made from things in nature. As time went on, our instruments became more advanced.

Today, there are many choices! There are just three main types: percussion, string, and wind.

Percussion instruments are probably the oldest. They are played by being struck, shaken, or rubbed. A drum is an example of a percussion instrument.

String instruments produce sound when their strings vibrate. They can either be plucked or played with a bow. Violins and guitars are examples of stringed instruments.

Wind instruments produce sound when air is blown into them or across them. Early wind instruments were used during war to alert troops. An example is a trumpet.

You can find musical instruments in every culture and place. But you might notice differences. For example, the Caribbean steel drum is made from a metal barrel. The drum is shaped like a bowl and played with rubber topped sticks. Bongo drums are made from wood shaped almost like a cone. They are held between the knees. Players strike them with their fingers.

It is fun to explore the many different types of instruments throughout the world and throughout history. You can make many of these instruments at home. This book tells you how using simple materials from around your house or at school.

Xylophone

Are You Ready?

The first xylophones were just loose wood bars placed on someone's legs. The musician would strike the bars with sticks to make sounds. Because each bar was a different length, it produced a different sound. Today's xylophones are mounted to a backing, such as felt or rubber. They are made not only from wood but also from metal and other materials. Here is how to make a type of xylophone out of glass. **Remember to just tap the glass.**

Get Set

✓ **long piece of felt or cloth**

✓ **6 empty glass jars, any size**

✓ **puff paint (optional)**

✓ **ribbon (optional)**

✓ **water**

✓ **food coloring (optional)**

✓ **unsharpened pencil, craft stick, or chopstick**

✓ **metal spoon**

Let's Go!

1. On the felt, arrange the jars in one long line so there is about 2 inches in between each jar (see A). If you wish, tie ribbon around each jar and decorate (see B).

2. Fill the first jar with just enough water to cover the bottom of the jar. Fill the next jar with a little more water. Continue filling each jar with a little more water, so the last jar is almost full.

3. If you wish, add a few drops of food coloring to the water in each jar.

4. Use an unsharpened pencil, craft stick, or chopstick to gently tap each jar (see C). Notice how the sounds change from jar to jar.

5. Next, try the metal spoon. Tap the jars gently. What sounds can you make?

A

B

C

Rhythm Blocks

Are You Ready?

Sometimes music can be made from simply rubbing or tapping two surfaces together. That is the case with rhythm blocks. You may have seen this wooden instrument played in folk bands. You can make your own! The sandpaper makes many different sounds.

Get Set

- ✔ marker
- ✔ 2 small cereal boxes
- ✔ sandpaper
- ✔ scissors
- ✔ tacky craft glue
- ✔ poster paint (optional)
- ✔ paintbrush (optional)

Let's Go!

1. With the marker, trace the shape of each small cereal box on the sandpaper (see A). (See page 28 for the pattern.) Cut out both shapes.

2. Ask an adult for help. Apply tacky craft glue to one side of each box.

3. Place the sandpaper, smooth side down, onto the box. Do the same with the other piece of sandpaper. Trim the sandpaper edges if needed (see B). Let dry.

4. If you wish, paint the sides of the box that are not covered with sandpaper (see C). Let dry.

5. Once everything is dry, rub the sandpaper sides together. Listen to the sound. Now try tapping them against each other. Try your favorite rhythms.

A

NEW INSTANT GREAT GRUEL

300 g

B

C

Panpipes

Are You Ready?

Panpipes were played in ancient times. They are considered the first version of the harmonica, flute, and pipe organ.

The secret to playing a panpipe is in knowing where to blow. The bottom is usually sealed with wax. That means you cannot blow into the pipes to make a sound. You must blow across the top.

Get Set

✔ **10 drinking straws**

✔ **masking tape**

✔ **scissors**

✔ **modeling clay or play dough**

✔ **feathers (optional)**

✔ **stickers (optional)**

✔ **ribbon (optional)**

Let's Go!

1. Line up ten drinking straws. Tape the straws together about an inch from the top using masking tape (see A).

2. Cut the bottom of the straws in different lengths so they look like steps (see B). Fill the holes on the "step" side with small balls of modeling clay (see C). Leave the straight side open so you will be able to play it.

3. If you wish, decorate the pipe with feathers, stickers, or other decorations (see D).

4. To play the pipe, blow across the top of the straight and open edge. Go from side to side like a harmonica. Listen carefully. The sound will be quiet but you can hear it change in pitch.

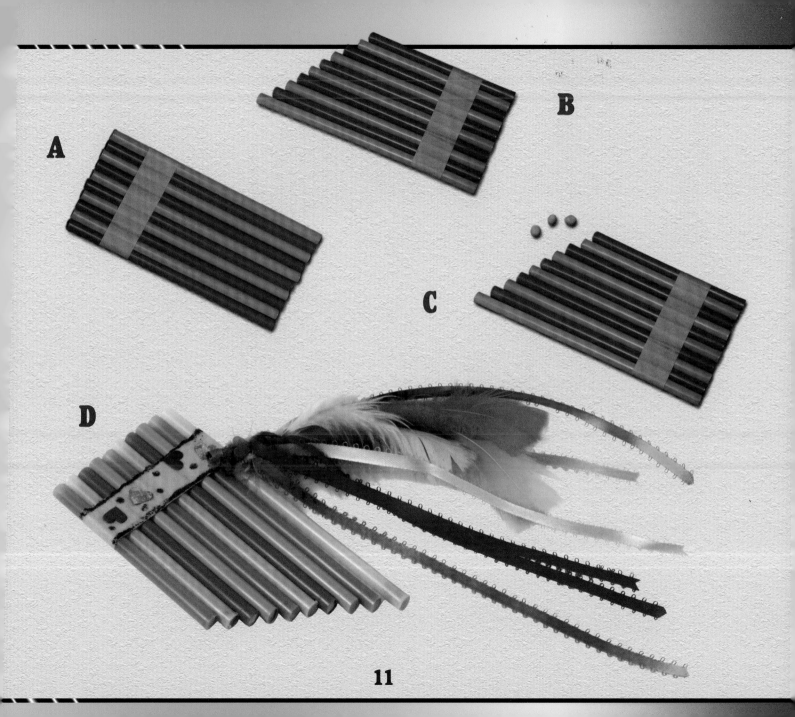

Finger Cymbals

Are You Ready?

Have you ever seen Middle Eastern dancers? They use finger cymbals to produce a number of different tones. The dancers wear these metal disks on the thumb and middle finger of each hand. They strike and ring them together in a pattern. Try it. You can follow the main melody, the drum beat, or find your own rhythm.

Get Set

✔ **elastic**

✔ **ruler**

✔ **scissors**

✔ **2 metal jar lids or bottle caps, washed and dried**

✔ **white glue**

✔ **masking tape**

✔ **puff paint (optional)**

Let's Go!

1. Measure and cut two pieces of elastic about 3-inches long.

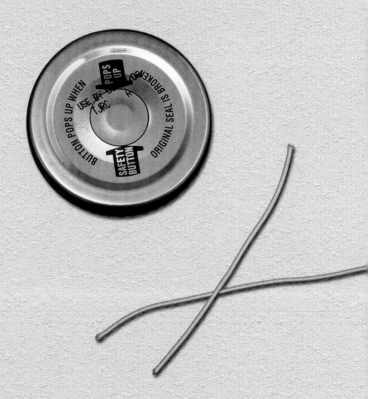

12

2. Make a loop with one piece of elastic and glue the ends to the inside of the metal jar lid. Do the same with the other piece of elastic and other lid. Let dry. Use a small piece of masking tape to make sure the elastic stays in place. If you wish, decorate the lids.

3. Put one cymbal on your thumb. Put the other cymbal on your middle finger of the same hand. You are ready to follow a beat!

Colonial Drum

Are You Ready?

In Colonial times, drummers marched with the soldiers during times of war. They were usually between the ages of twelve and sixteen and kept the soldiers together as they marched.

Get Set

- ✔ balloon
- ✔ scissors
- ✔ coffee or soup can, washed and dried
- ✔ duct tape
- ✔ construction paper (optional)
- ✔ glitter (optional)
- ✔ white glue (optional)
- ✔ markers (optional)
- ✔ rope or yarn
- ✔ 2 unsharpened pencils, chopsticks, or straws

Let's Go!

1. Ask an adult to blow up the balloon. Let the air out. This will help to stretch it. Cut straight across the balloon, cutting off the bottom (see A). Stretch the balloon tightly across the open part of the coffee or soup can so it covers the opening. Use duct tape to tape the edges down (see B). Ask an adult to help you so the balloon stays tight.

2. If you wish, carefully decorate the can. Glue construction paper around the can. Let dry. Use glitter or markers to decorate the paper. Let dry.

3. Measure a piece of rope or yarn by loosely wrapping it twice around your waist. Place the middle of the rope around the can and tie a knot (see C). Use the ends of the rope to make a bow around your waist.

4. Try a few rhythms with the pencils, chopsticks, or straws. You are ready to march!

14

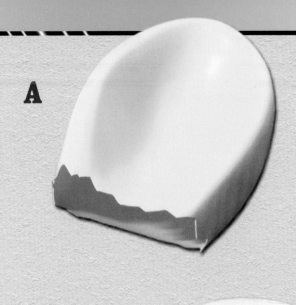

A

B

C

American Indian Clapper

When you think of American Indian dances, you probably think of drums. But American Indians first learned about drums from the Europeans. Before that, they used clappers to keep rhythm. A clapper was made by splitting a branch partway down the center. By hitting the clapper against their hands, it made a sound. Here is an easy way to make a clapper without having to chop down a tree!

Get Set

- ✔ pencil
- ✔ 2 lids from a frozen juice can
- ✔ cardboard from a cereal box
- ✔ scissors
- ✔ white glue
- ✔ masking tape
- ✔ 2 craft sticks
- ✔ markers (optional)

Let's Go!

1. With a pencil, trace the shape of each lid on the cardboard (see page 26 for the pattern). Cut out the two circles (see A).

2. Glue or tape one circle to one lid (see B). Do the same with the other circle and lid. Let dry.

3. Glue or tape one craft stick to the cardboard side of each lid. Let dry.

4. Position the sticks so the lids face each other. Tape the bottom of the craft sticks together (see C).

5. If you wish, decorate the cardboard side and craft sticks of the clapper using markers or other decorations (see D). Let dry.

6. Shake the clapper or hit it against your hand to make a sound.

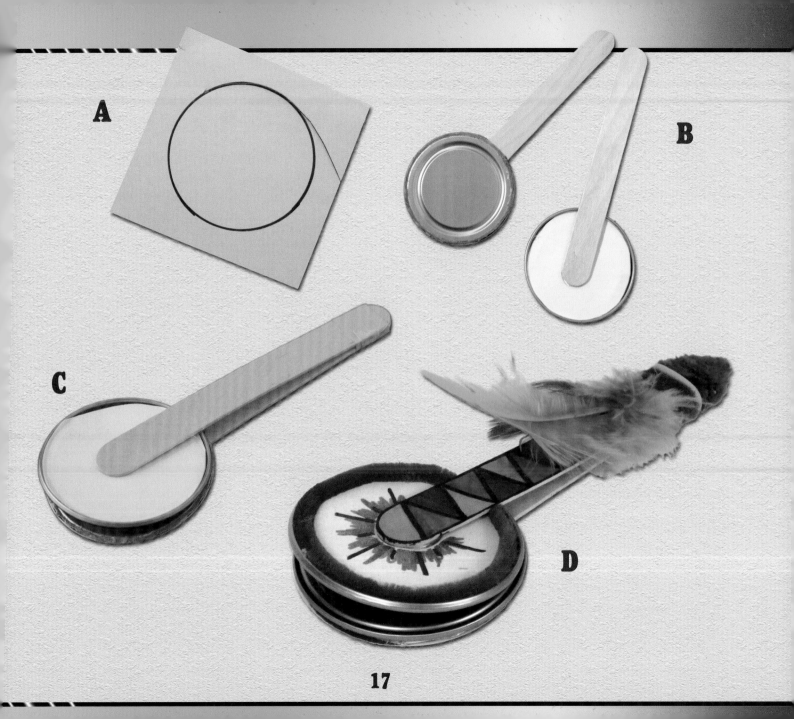

A

B

C

D

Tambourine

Are You Ready?

Long ago, someone thought about taking the top of a drum and adding jingles. This new instrument became a tambourine. Tambourines have been used since ancient times. Today, they are used in gospel, pop, and rock and roll music. Try playing your tambourine by shaking it or striking it against your palm, leg, or hip.

Get Set

✔ **marker**

✔ **1 disposable aluminum pie plate**

✔ **ruler**

✔ **hole punch**

✔ **5 pipe cleaners or 10 twist ties**

✔ **scissors**

✔ **20 1-inch metal washers or 10 medium-sized jingle bells**

✔ **ribbon (optional)**

Let's Go!

1. With the marker, make sixteen evenly spaced dots around the edge of a pie plate. Use the hole punch to punch out the holes. Ask an adult for help.

Safety Note:
Be sure to ask for help from an adult, if needed, to complete these crafts!

18

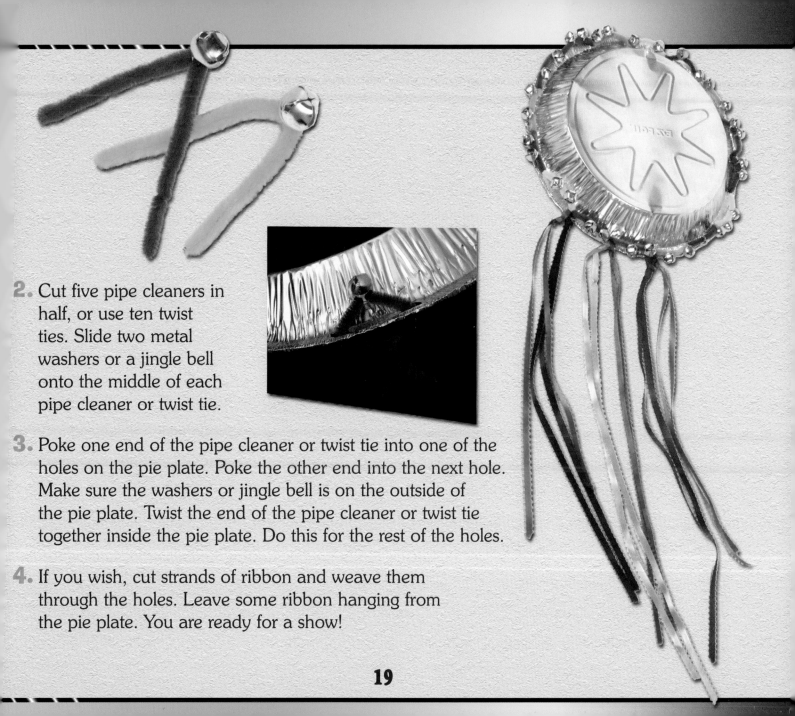

2. Cut five pipe cleaners in half, or use ten twist ties. Slide two metal washers or a jingle bell onto the middle of each pipe cleaner or twist tie.

3. Poke one end of the pipe cleaner or twist tie into one of the holes on the pie plate. Poke the other end into the next hole. Make sure the washers or jingle bell is on the outside of the pie plate. Twist the end of the pipe cleaner or twist tie together inside the pie plate. Do this for the rest of the holes.

4. If you wish, cut strands of ribbon and weave them through the holes. Leave some ribbon hanging from the pie plate. You are ready for a show!

Rain Stick

Are You Ready?

Rain sticks produce a sound like falling rain drops. They are still used by Indians in Mexico, South America, and the Southwestern United States to try to bring rain. Whether or not they affect the weather, these sticks make a gentle rain-like sound. Originally made from a dried cactus branch filled with pebbles, rain sticks can also be made from some common materials.

Get Set

- ✔ **aluminum foil**
- ✔ **paper towel roll**
- ✔ **ruler**
- ✔ **scissors**
- ✔ **clear tape**
- ✔ **1 cup uncooked rice**
- ✔ **feathers (optional)**
- ✔ **glitter (optional)**
- ✔ **markers (optional)**

Let's Go!

1. Squeeze a piece of 12-inch × 12-inch aluminum foil into a long snake-like shape (see pattern on page 27). Coil the foil snake so it looks like a spring (see A). Make it narrow enough to fit in the paper towel roll. Put the foil spring into the paper towel roll. It should fill the paper towel roll from top to bottom. If it does not, add another coiled foil snake.

2. Cut out two 4-inch × 4-inch squares of foil (see pattern on page 26). Cover one end of the tube with one square of foil (see B). Use clear tape to tape the foil in place.

3. Pour in 1 cup of uncooked rice (see C).

4. Cover the open end of the tube with the second square of foil. Use clear tape to tape the foil in place.

5. If you wish, decorate the rain stick using feathers, glitter, and markers (see D). Let dry.

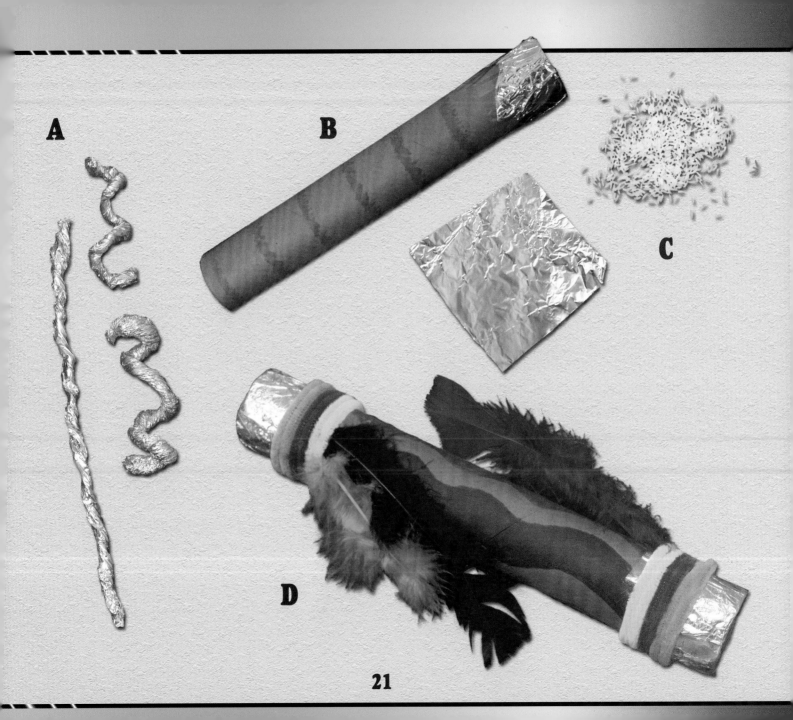

A

B

C

D

21

Maracas

Are You Ready?

Maracas were first used by Puerto Ricans. They made them out of a small fruit called the higuera. The dried-out shell was filled with pebbles and attached to a handle. Modern maracas are made out of plastic or wood. Today, this percussion instrument adds an exciting rhythm to salsa music.

Get Set

- ✔ **2 empty frozen juice cans with lids, washed and dried**
- ✔ **uncooked corn, rice, or dried beans**
- ✔ **light cardboard**
- ✔ **scissors**
- ✔ **hole punch**
- ✔ **pencil**
- ✔ **2 unsharpened pencils**
- ✔ **masking tape**
- ✔ **tissue paper, any color**
- ✔ **white glue**
- ✔ **paintbrush**
- ✔ **glue wash (1 part white glue, 1 part water)**

Let's Go!

1. Remove one lid from one juice can (see A). Fill the can one third of the way with uncooked corn, rice, or dried beans.

2. Trace the lid of the juice can onto a piece of cardboard. Cut it out. Ask an adult to carefully punch a hole in the center of the circle.

3. Fit the unsharpened pencil through the hole. Place the cardboard with the pencil on the open end of the juice can. Use masking tape to secure the cardboard to the juice can (see B).

4. Tear tissue paper into different sizes. Put the juice can down with the pencil sticking up. Brush glue onto the juice can and a little bit of the pencil. Place the tissue paper pieces all over the glue. Be sure to overlap the pieces. Let dry. Cover the top of the can with glue and cover with tissue paper (see C). Let dry. Brush a glue wash over the entire can. Let dry.

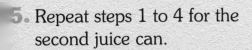

5. Repeat steps 1 to 4 for the second juice can.

6. Give the dry juice cans a gentle shake. You are now ready to play a salsa rhythm!

A

B

C

23

Ukulele

Although invented by Portuguese craftsmen, the ukulele was very popular in Hawaii. It looks just like a small, four-stringed guitar. Its name means "jumping flea" because that is how fingers look when they play it. They seem to fly from string to string.

Get Set

- ✔ cereal box
- ✔ pencil
- ✔ scissors
- ✔ paper towel roll
- ✔ poster paint
- ✔ paintbrush
- ✔ markers
- ✔ 4 long rubber bands (and some extras in case they break)
- ✔ masking tape

Let's Go!

1. Draw a circle or oval on the cereal box. Carefully cut out the circle or oval (see A). Ask an adult for help.

2. Using poster paint, paint the cereal box and paper towel roll. Let dry. Use markers to make any design that you wish (see pattern on page 29). Let dry.

3. Stretch four long rubber bands so they fit over the box the long way (see B). Pluck a band to see how it sounds.

4. Take the paper towel roll. Carefully, cut two slits along the bottom about 2-inches long. Fold back the sides.

5. Press the sides against one end of the box to make a handle. Tape the sides down using masking tape. Use markers or poster paint to cover the masking tape. Let dry (see C).

6. Now pluck the bands. How can you make the sounds different?

A

B

C

300 g

Patterns

Use tracing paper to copy the patterns on these pages. Ask an adult to help you cut and trace the shapes onto construction paper.

American Indian Clapper
at 100%

Rain Stick at 100%
(cut from aluminum
foil, 4 × 4-inches)

Rain Stick enlarge 200%
(cut from aluminum foil, 12 × 12-inches)

Rhythm Blocks
at 100%

Ukulele at 100%

Reading About

Books

Aliki. *Ah, Music!* New York: HarperCollins, 2003.

Dubois, Muriel L. *I Like Music: What Can I Be?* Mankato, Minn.: Bridgestone Books, 2001.

Krull, Kathleen. *M is for Music.* Orlando, Fla.: Harcourt, 2003.

Levine, Robert. *The Story of the Orchestra: Listen While You Learn About the Instruments, the Music, and the Composers Who Wrote the Music.* New York: Black Dog and Leventhal, 2001.